LEEK & MANIFOLD VALLEY LIGHT RAILWAY

Lindsey Porter

Ashbourne Editions

INTRODUCTION

Most days of the year, even when the weather is bad, visitors can be found walking and cycling along the Manifold and Hamps Valleys between Waterhouses in the south and Hulme End in the north. It is a distance of eight miles and the path they use is covered with tarmac.

It is the track bed of the Leek & Manifold Valley Light Railway, which ran between 1904 and 1934. Several books have been written about the history of the line. Yet for those who are not ardent railway enthusiasts, there is currently no title in print which satisfies the casual visitor's curiosity. This book's object is to satisfy that need. With the use of period photographs, chiefly of the railway but also of nearby villages, the days of the L&MVLR are brought back for us.

The popularity today of this little line stems perhaps because of the nostalgia for things gone by and its superb location. It must also be because of the unusual nature of the railway. It was narrow gauge, built to a rail width of thirty inches. The engines were of a very similar design to those on the Barsi Light Railway in India. Even the coaches were colonial in style. They were painted primrose yellow and must have been quite picturesque when seen down the valley.

This collection of photographs will, I hope, give a good pictorial record of what there was and what could have been today, had the line survived the years of the Depression and the war that followed it. I hope you enjoy them.

Lindsey Porter

© C.L.M. Porter 1995
ACKNOWLEDGEMENTS
I wish to thank Derbyshire Life & Countryside of Derby for use of their photo of the train at Beeston Tor, Robert Cartwright (page 61) and Basil Jeuda for the Nithsdale postcard of three valley scenes. The cover was painted by Tony Beresford of Underhill Farm, Buxton Road, Longnor, near Buxton, Derbyshire SK17 0PU. Designed by Dick Richardson.

The right of C.L.M. Porter as author of this work has been asserted by him in accordance with the Copyright, Designs and Patents Act, 1993.

Bitish Library Cataloguing in Publication Data: A catalogue record for this book is available from the British Library.

Printed in England by J.W. Arrowsmith, Bristol.

THE BEGINNINGS

The number of documents associated with the establishment of the railway was perhaps more than may be realised. Here are a selection. Some relate to operating, borrowing, as well as the shares prospectus, etc. *(Overleaf).*

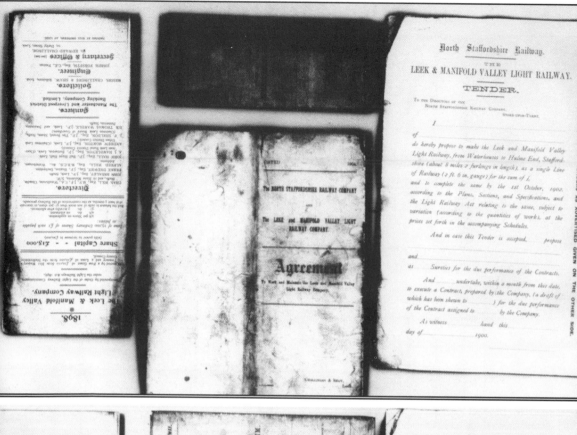

Construction of Swainsley Tunnel. The locomotive is 0-4-2 **Skylark**, built in 1902 by Kerr Stuart and Co. Ltd., of Stoke-on-Trent. It ended its days on the Snailbeach District Railway in Shropshire where it was scrapped in May 1950.

Above: Construction of the bridge over the road at the rear of the Crown Inn, Waterhouses. The lower photo shows the line to this bridge. There was a delay in the construction of the line from Leek and it would appear from these photos that the Waterhouses end was laid with narrow gauge track during construction work.

One of the two engines was named after Everard R. Calthrop *(left)*, the chief engineer who was involved in light railway construction at the Welshpool and Llanfair Railway in Wales and also on the Barsi Light Railway in India, where a loco similar to the Manifold engines has been preserved. The other engine was named after John B. Earle, the resident engineer *(below left)*. Also featured here is Godfrey Brewer, the mechanical engineer.

Hulme End Station on open day, 27th June, 1904. The station waiting room and ticket office. The middle building was the engine shed with the coach shed on the right. A water tower dominated the scene and other features were added after the opening including an old coach body for parcels and bikes, and a coal bunker. The coach shed appears to have been initially open sided. The platform was only 6" high.

Above: The coach shed, engine, and one of the two low-sided bogie wagons (the other is behind it), used to transport guests on the open day. The seats are from the various stations, four to a wagon, with those from Beeston Tor and Grindon in view. Only two carriages had been delivered ahead of the opening.

Below: One of the ceremonial arches erected at Waterhouses on open day. It says *'Welcome to Earl Dartmouth'*, the Lord Lieutenant of Staffordshire, who performed the opening ceremony.

Waterhouses

Above: Because of the delay in the connecting line to Leek, a temporary station was built near where the line crossed the Ashbourne-Leek road. Here is the telegraph office and the steam bus which brought passengers from Leek.

Below: The open day train entering the Hamps Valley with both engines in steam.

Ready for traffic: *Above:* Grindon Station with a spur to a section of standard gauge line. *Below left:* Approaching Thor's Cave and, *Below right:* Swainsley Tunnel from the bridge over the Warslow Brook.

THE STRAKER STEAM BUSES

The line from Leek was not opened until 1st July, 1905, and so for the first year of operations the NSR used two steam buses built by Straker and Co., of Bristol. They had iron-tyred wheels and the excessive vibration resulted in them being nicknamed **Earthquake 1 and 2.** They broke gas mantles in neighbouring properties and were restricted to Ashbourne Road, Heywood Street, Brook Street and Broad Street while in Leek. One of them was later converted to a removal van in Burslem, Stoke-on-Trent.

Above: Boarding at Leek Station (rear right). *Below:* Approaching the bus stop (see next photo) at the bottom of Ashbourne Road, Leek.

Above: Loading up outside the Talbot Hotel, Leek. Passengers boarded at the rear. *Below:* There were three services a day and four on Thursday and Saturday. Here is E223 at Lowe Hill Bridge near Leek. The bus used to frighten horses, necessitating the drivers to dismount and hold the bridle, as is happening here.

Leek Station in a snow storm, taken at about the time the Waterhouses line opened.

Facing page above: The bus at Waterhouses outside the Crown Inn.
Facing page below: On the railway bridge in Church Street, Ashbourne.

One of the early trains at Bradnop Station after the Leek-Waterhouses line had been opened and the steam buses finally replaced.

TIMETABLES

North Staffordshire Railway.

LEEK & WATERHOUSES
OMNIBUS SERVICE

COMMENCING JUNE 29th, and until AUGUST 31st.

The Motor Omnibus, in connection with the Trains on the Manifold Valley Light Railway, will run between Leek and Waterhouses in connection with Trains to and from the North Staffordshire System, as shewn below :--

TIME TABLE.

	a.m.	a.m.	Thursdays and Saturdays only P.M.	Thursdays and Saturdays Excepted P.M.	Thursdays and Saturdays only P.M.		a.m.	p.m.	p.m.	Thursdays and Saturdays only P.M.
Leek - - - dep.	8 50	11 15	2 15	5 0	7 25	Waterhouses - dep.	10 5	12 35	6 15	8 40
Bradnop - about	9 8	11 33	2 33	5 18	7 43	Winkhill - about	10 20	12 50	6 30	8 55
Bottom House ,,	9 26	11 51	2 51	5 36	8 1	Bottom House ,,	10 24	12 54	6 34	9 0
Winkhill - - ,,	9 30	11 55	2 55	5 40	8 5	Bradnop - - ,,	10 42	1 12	6 52	9 18
Waterhouses - arr.	9 50	12 15	3 15	6 0	8 25	Leek - - arr.	11 5	1 35	7 15	9 40

Passengers will be allowed to take luggage not exceeding 28 lbs. without charge at their own risk. Packages exceeding 28 lbs. will not be conveyed.

The Motor Omnibus will accommodate 22 Passengers only, and not more than that number can be accepted for conveyance ; and in all cases preference will be given to Passengers arriving and going forward by Train.

Stoke-on-Trent, June, 1904.

W. D. PHILLIPPS, General Manager.

Harry Lockett, Printer, Hanley.

The poster announcing the bus service issued in June 1904.

NORTH STAFFORDSHIRE RAILWAY.

THE MANIFOLD VALLEY LIGHT RAILWAY

WILL BE OPENED FOR TRAFFIC

On Wednesday, June 29th, 1904

Train Service: Week Days only.

Miles from Leek		First and Third Class only					Fares Third Class from Leek
		a.m.	a.m.	p.m.	p.m.	p.m.	
8	Leek (Railway Station) dep. by Motor Omnibus	8 50	11 15	2 15	5 0	7 25	8d.
	Waterhouses arr.	9 50	12 15	3 15	6 0	8 25	

Miles from Waterhouses		First and Third Class only					Fares Third Class from Waterhouses single / return
	Waterhouses dep.	10 5	12 30	3 30	6 15	8 40	
2	Sparrowlee	10 13	12 38	3 38	6 23	8 48	2d. 3d.
4	Beeston Tor	10 23	12 45	3 48	6 34	8 55	4d. 7d.
4	Grindon	10 28	12 51	3 51	6 37	9 1	4d. 7d.
5	Thor's Cave	10 31	12 56	3 56	6 43	9 6	5d. 8d.
6	Wetton Mill	10 36	1 1	4 1	6 48	9 11	6d. 10d.
7	Butterton	10 42	1 7	4 7	6 55	9 17	7d. 1/-
8	Ecton (for Warslow)	10 45	1 10	4 10	6 59	9 20	8d. 1/1
9	Hulme End (for Hartington) arr	10 50	1 15	4 15	7 5	9 25	9d. 1/3

Miles from Hulme End		First and Third Class only					Fares Third Class from Hulme End single / return
		a.m.	a.m.	p.m.	p.m.	p.m.	
	Hulme End (for Hartington) dep	9 5	11 35	2 30	5 10	7 40	
1	Ecton (for Warslow)	9 10	11 40	2 35	5 16	7 45	1d. 2d.
2	Butterton	9 13	11 43	2 38	5 20	7 48	2d. 3d.
3	Wetton Mill	9 19	11 49	2 44	5 27	7 54	3d. 5d.
4	Thor's Cave	9 24	11 54	2 49	5 32	7 59	4d. 7d.
5	Grindon	9 29	11 59	2 54	5 38	8 4	5d. 8d.
5	Beeston Tor	9 32	12 2	2 57	5 41	8 7	5d. 8d.
7	Sparrowlee	9 42	12 12	3 7	5 52	8 17	7d. 1/-
9	Waterhouses arr	9 50	12 20	3 15	6 0	8 25	9d. 1/3

Miles from Waterhouses							Fares from Waterhouses
	Waterhouses dep. by Motor Omnibus	10 5	12 35		6 15	8 40	
8	Leek (Railway Station) arr.	11 5	1 35		7 15	9 40	8d.

● Thursdays and Saturdays only, Motor Omnibus and Train. ✗ Thursdays and Saturdays excepted, Motor Omnibus only.

N.B.—The Motor Omnibus will carry 22 Passengers, and only that number will be accepted for conveyance; and in all cases preference will be given to Passengers arriving or going forward by Railway.

MARKET TICKETS

will be issued to **LEEK** on WEDNESDAYS and SATURDAYS at Reduced Fares, viz.:

From Hulme End 1s.6d., all other Stations 1s.3d., Third Class.

LUGGAGE.—Holders of Market Tickets are permitted to carry Baskets or other Packages containing Eggs, Butter, Fruit, or other Market Produce, at their Own Risk, not exceeding 28 lbs. in weight, without charge. Packages exceeding 28 lbs. 1/- per cwt. with no less charge than 6d. But the Company hereby give notice that they are not and will not be responsible for any article so conveyed by Passengers. If required to be conveyed at the Company's Risk, Ordinary Rates will be charged.

On MONDAYS, THURSDAYS and SATURDAYS, Cheap Excursion Tickets will be issued at STOKE Station to Hulme End or any intermediate Station.

Fare 3/- for the Double Journey.

Important Notice to Cyclists.

Free Storage (at the owner's risk) will be provided for the day at Waterhouses, for the Cycles of parties arriving there by road and proceeding by rail to any Station on the Manifold Valley Railway.

Scale of Parcels Rates.

Parcels between Leek and Waterhouses or Hulme End, and intermediate points, will be charged as follows:—

Not exceeding			10 lbs.	6d. each.
Above 10 and not exceeding	20 "			8d. "
" 20 " "	28 "			10d. "

Parcels weighing above 28 lbs. will not be accepted for conveyance on the Omnibus.

LUGGAGE.—Ordinary Passengers are allowed to carry 40lbs. weight free all being personal luggage and not goods, merchandise, or other articles carried for sale, hire or profit.

W. D. PHILLIPPS, General Manager.

HARRY LOCKETT, PRINTER, HANLEY.

The poster for the line itself. It cost 1s 3d return between Waterhouses and Hulme End.

North Staffordshire Railway and Commercial Cars Company, Limited.

PLEASURE TRIPS
TO
BUXTON
BY RAIL AND MOTOR CHAR-A-BANC.
Via the Manifold Valley "Toy" Railway.

EVERY MONDAY, WEDNESDAY & SATURDAY,
Until September 25th,

A Motor Char-a-banc service will be run by the Commercial Cars Co., Limited. (London), between Hulme End and Buxton at the times and in connection with the Trains shown below.

From		At	
		a.m.	a.m.
STOKE	dep.	8 10	8 50
LEEK	"	8 50	10 55
HULME END	arr.	10 15	12 10
"	dep.	10 20	1 15
BUXTON (MARKET PLACE)	arr.	11 30	2 15

B Saturdays only.

From		At B	At J		p.m.
		p.m.	p.m.		p.m.
BUXTON (MARKET PLACE)	dep.	12 0	1 0		5 0
HULME END	arr.	1 0	1 35		6 15
"	dep.		1 50		7 30
LEEK	"	3 0	3 40		
STOKE	arr.	4 18	4 18		8 13

J Mondays and Wednesdays.

Motor Char-a-banc fares between Hulme End and Buxton Single Journey, 2/-, Return, 3/-

In connection with the Char-a-banc service Day Excursion Tickets will be issued from Stoke to Hulme End at a fare of **2/6**, and from Leek to Hulme End at a fare of **1/8**. Children under 12 years of age, Half-price.

With a view to ensuring accommodation on the Motor Char-a-bancs Passengers are invited to advise the Chief Booking Clerks at Stoke and Leek Stations respectively by post-card the previous night of their intention to make the journey.

The issuing of Tickets in connection with these Pleasure Trips is subject to the conditions and regulations referred to in the Time Tables, Bills and Notices of the respective Companies on whose Railways, Coaches or Cars they are available, and the respective Companies will not be liable for any loss or damage, injury, delay, or detention to the person or property of the holder caused or arising out of their respective Railway. The contract and liability of each Company are limited to its own Railway, Coaches or Cars.

W. D. PHILLIPPS, General Manager.

Station Office, Stoke, September, 1909.

HARRY LOCKETT, PRINTER, HANLEY.

The Commercial Cars, Limited.

A NEW ATTRACTION FOR BUXTON !!!

MOTOR TOURS
For Residents and Visitors.

Road and Rail Pleasure Trips by Motor Char-a-banc and Train over the "Toy" Railway running through the beautiful

MANIFOLD VALLEY

Every MONDAY, WEDNESDAY & SATURDAY,
Until September 25th.

A service of well-appointed Char-a-Bancs will run between Buxton and Hulme End. The Cars will run from the Market Place at the times shown below to Hulme End in connection with the Trains on the Toy Railway through the beautiful and far-famed Manifold Valley.

Char-a-banc Fares Single Journey 2/-, Return 3/-

In connection with these Tours, Cheap Return Tickets will be issued by the Railway Co. at Hulme End for the full length of the Manifold Valley Line (about 9 miles) to Waterhouses, also to Leek and Stoke-on-Trent by the Trains and at the Fares shown.

From		At B	At J	noon	
		a.m.	noon		
Buxton (Market Place)	dep.	9 30	12 0	1 30	1 50
Hulme End	arr.	10 30	1 0	1 54	1 57

From		At			p.m.
		a.m.			p.m.
Hulme End	dep.	10 35	1 35		4 5
Ecton (Wetton)	"	10 39	1 38		5 15
Butterton	"	10 42	1 44		5 30
Wetton Mill	"	10 49	1 49		5 34
Thor's Cave	"	10 53	1 53		5 37
Grindon	"	10 58	1 58		5 44
Beeston Tor	"	11 0	2 0		5 58
Sparrowlee	"	11 10	2 10		6 5
Waterhouses	arr.	11 15	2 15		6 15

From		At			p.m.
Waterhouses	dep.	11 33	3 30		
Leek	arr.	11 49			
Stoke-on-Trent	"	12 8			

Return Fare from Hulme End to Waterhouses ... 1/3
" " " to Leek ... 1/8
" " " to Stoke-on-Trent ... 2/8

Children under 12 years of age, Half-price.

The Railway Tickets will be available for Passengers to alight from or join the Train at any of the halts on the Manifold Valley Line.

The Commercial Cars, Limited.

Cambridge Street, London, W.C., September 1st, 1909.

HARRY LOCKETT, PRINTER, HANLEY.

Posters for the charabanc service between Buxton Station and Hulme End, issued in 1909.

ROLLING STOCK

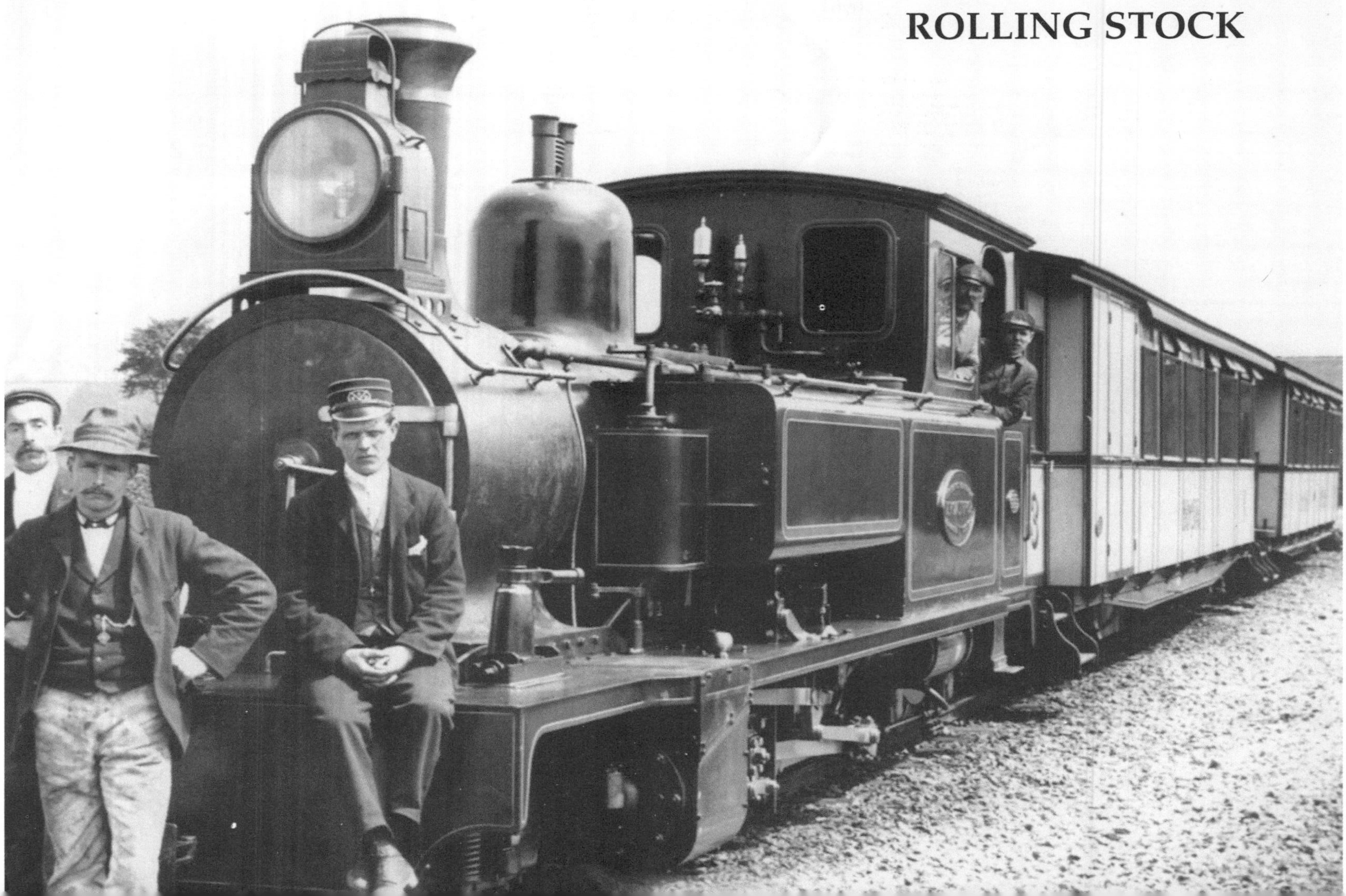

The ex-works photo of **E.R. Calthrop.**

Facing page: The engines were 2-6-4 T's built by Kitson and Co., of Leeds. Initially they were chocolate brown and the coaches primrose yellow. This photo was probably taken on the opening day. The man in the trilby is J.B. Earle standing in front of **E.R. Calthrop.**

A damaged photo taken from The Tramway and Railway World of 1904 showing **J.B. Earle** , the transporter car and carriage. The transporter allowed standard gauge rolling stock to be carried up the 2'6" gauge line and was designed by E.R. Calthrop and first used on any narrow gauge system here on the Manifold Line.

Facing page: **E.R. Calthrop** at Hulme End. *(Real Photos).*

Probably **E.R. Calthrop** outside the engine shed and adjacent to the booking office at Hulme End. The travelling crane on the right allowed some repair work to be done on site. Bigger jobs meant taking the engines to Stoke and later to Crewe. (*Real Photos*).

E.R. Calthrop after being returned from Crewe the 'wrong way round'.

A further view of **E.R. Calthrop** at Hulme End coupled to the transporter and two carriages in LMS crimson livery. (*Real Photos*).

The two engines together after the switch. Despite fears to the contrary, **E.R. Calthrop** (on the right), served just as well. (*Real Photos*).

J.B. Earle with the four carriages at Hulme End. (*Real Photos*).

J.B. Earle coaled up with about one ton of coal. The coal bunker on both engines was increased in height as can be clearly seen here.

Facing Page: Both engines adjacent to the coaling bunker. On the left is one of the 1st/3rd class composite coaches and one of the low-side wagons loaded with milk churns. *(Real Photos).*

Above: **J.B. Earle** at the entrance to Hulme End Station. There were two height gauges, the other being off to the left of this photo. *(Photomatic).*

Facing page: **J.B. Earle** (in front of E.R. Calthrop) taking on water. (Real Photos).

Below: A double headed train with the open wagons converted for carrying passengers. This was usually on Bank Holidays, although the Gorsedd ceremonies held at Thor's Cave in September 1925 to at least 1928 attracted huge crowds of upwards of 2,000 from 1926 onwards. Extra trains were run to cope with the demand!

Above: Driver and mate on **J.B. Earle.** *Below:* The same loco pulling a coal wagon of standard gauge on the transporter at Hulme End.

Ex works photo of the coaches. There were two sorts; a third class only coach, with the open platforms at each end, and a first and third class composite coach. The latter had the platform only at the first class end, with a guard's compartment at the other end. The coaches were 42 feet long, 10 feet high and 8 feet wide. The width of the carriages was a bold move given the 2'6" gauge, but all worked well and the passengers were conveyed in more comfort. There were a total of four coaches, two of each type.

A further view of the third class carriage looking through the open door to the platform.

Facing page: The interior of the coaches showing first class *(above)* and third class (*below).* The composite carried 8 first class and 20 third class passengers, while the third class only coaches carried forty people.

A close-up of the composite coach in LMS red livery. The ornate logo L & MVLR was painted over and the vehicle given the LMS number 14989. Note the brake on the platform of the adjoining coach. (*Photomatic*).

The transporter wagon with a standard gauge goods wagon. (*Photomatic*).

Approaching *Waterhouses* Station in 1926 with a composite coach and one of the low-sided wagons loaded with milk churns. The carriage of churns appears to have been their principal use except when carrying passengers on Bank Holidays. (*L & GRP*).

A view at Hulme End of the transporter car carrying a standard gauge wagon. These appeared in The Tramway and Railway World in July 1904. This simple idea enabled standard gauge stock to be carried and rolled off onto standard gauge metals at all stations except Beeston Tor and Redhurst Halt. The difference in height of the two rails was ten inches. To load the car, a lever was pulled which locked the car. The standard gauge vehicle was pushed on by hand and its wheels secured by screw wedges. The lever was returned and the car was then ready. It was intended that the car could also be used for carrying timber, milk churns, bulky items and interestingly, road vehicles.

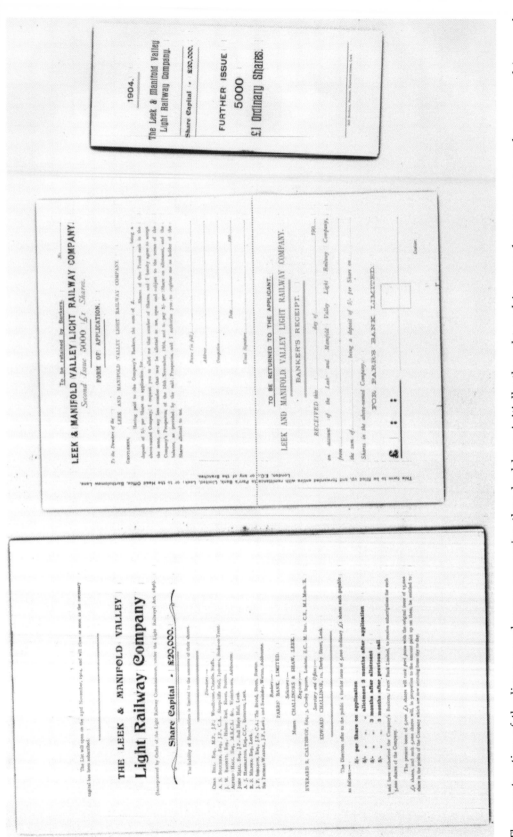

The construction of the line proved more expensive than had been initially thought and it proved necessary to make a second issue of shares. Here are the prospectus and application form. Additional to the £20,000 shares, the Company received a Treasury grant of £17,500, a Treasury loan of £7,500 and a County Council loan of £10,000 initially plus a further £5,000 received on 3rd January 1907.

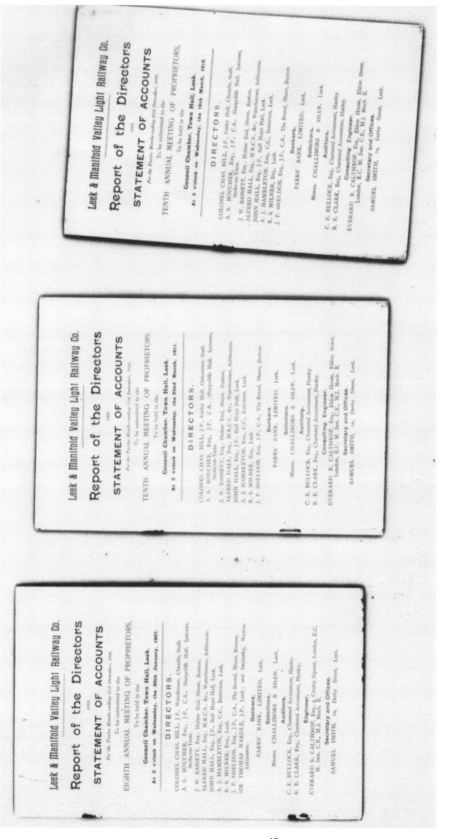

Examples of the AGM Reports of the Directors. The 1907 report indicates that at the end of 1906, the share issue had raised only £15,482. The number of passengers carried (in the year ending November) was:

	Single	Return
1905	10,347	19,149
1906	11,084	29,463
Increase	737	10,314

THE STATIONS

Waterhouses Station with the top of the steps which gave access to the platforms from the road. The signal box is in the background.

Facing page: The diminutive narrow gauge train at Waterhouses alongside the Leek train. The little building is the booking office and the ladies waiting room. Notice the chimney above the guard's compartment on the first Manifold coach! The larger engine is ex NSR No.53, 0-6-4T, renumbered 2042 by the LMS and withdrawn in 1935.

Ready for Hulme End, the coaches stand outside the Waterhouses cantilevered shelter. They are in LMS livery. The photo was taken in 1933.

On leaving Waterhouses Station, the train had to stop for the gates across the Leek-Ashbourne road. (*L & GRP*).

Above: Heading for home. A group of people walking from the station at Waterhouses into the village. *Below:* A wintry day at Waterhouses.

Two postcards of the line passing End Farm at the entrance to the Hamps Valley.

Nithsdale, a commercial photographer of Leek, took several photos of the train and surrounding villages and some of them are reproduced in this book. He produced a series of postcards consisting of three views, one of which was of the Manifold train. *(Basil Jeuda).*

Sparrowlee Station. Note the six inch high platform and the standard gauge siding in the inset photo.

Beeston Tor Station. An old coach body served as a shelter and it is visible beyond the train.

The beauty of the Manifold Valley above Weags Bridge and Grindon Station looking towards Beeston Tor with the line clearly visible *(above)*. Looking down towards Beeston Tor Station with the refreshment hut by the river Hamps *(below)*.

Former Light Railway, Manifold Valley

A lovely and rare photo at Beeston Tor showing all the coaches in service with extra seating on the low-sided wagons and a coal wagon at the rear *(above) Derbyshire Life & Countryside.* An earlier refreshment hut at Beeston Tor. This is a postcard postmarked 1909 *(below).*

Grindon Station with the standard gauge siding.

Weags Bridge with Grindon Station beyond *(above)*. During the summer, the river is usually dry between Wetton Mill and Ilam. This photo was taken from Weags Bridge and includes a wagon on the standard gauge siding.

A four coach set at Thor's Cave Station with the refreshment hut and waiting room.

Two further views of Thor's Cave Station. On the later and lower photo, a new refreshment hut is in place and toilets have been added behind the waiting room.

J.B. Earle pulls away from Thor's Cave Station *(above)*. Thor's Cave Station *(below)*. *L & GRP.*

Above: Beneath Thor's Cave, the train leaves for Waterhouses. *Below:* Wetton village some ninety years ago.

MANIFOLD LIGHT RAILWAY

The classic view of the train approaching Thor's Cave Station.

Above: Looking towards Redhurst Crossing. Redhurst Gorge from which the name was taken is off to the right of this photo. *Below:* Loading milk at Redhurst Crossing.

MANIFOLD VALLEY.

E.R. Calthrop leaving Redhurst Crossing for Thor's Cave. The first wagon carries the initials 'RH&S': it's a coal wagon from the coalmines of Robert Heath and Sons of Norton and Kidsgrove *(above)*. A double headed train chiefly lost in its own smoke between Wetton Mill and Redhurst Halt *(below)*.

Leaving Wetton Mill for Waterhouses the train passes Darfur Crags and the river swallets.

The view towards Wetton Mill farm from the Hoo brook footbridge, taken some ninety or so years ago.

on Mill Station, Manifold Valley, North Stafford Railway.

An old NSR postcard of the train at Wetton Mill *(above)*. Wetton Mill Station *(below)*.

Wetton Mill Bridge, built in 1807 by the Duke of Devonshire at a cost of £184 after the previous bridge was destroyed by flooding. The railway siding is visible on the right. The section of the river was impounded as the millpond for Wetton Mill.

Butterton at the beginning of the century. The cyclist is a Post Office telegram messenger.

Facing page: Two views of Grindon village at the beginning of the century. The upper view is close to the church and the lower one shows the village pub.

South of Swainsley Tunnel *(above)*. The south portal of the tunnel *(below)*.

J.B Earle approaching the tunnel at Swainsley *(above)*. Swainsley Hall, possibly taken in 1903 and certainly before 1911, when an east wing was added. Built in 1867 for a Mr Roscoe, a London solicitor, it was the home of Sir Thomas Wardle. He was a supporter of the line and a director too. However the railway incurred additional costs as the tunnel was built at his insistence.

Ecton Station with a temporary line in the foreground.

Facing page: The line at Ecton Lea, showing Naylor's Temperance Hotel. The field in the foreground was used as a bowling green for a time. Above the two huts at the side of this field may be seen a collection of huts used by the navvies during the construction of the line. There was an outbreak of smallpox here in February 1903 affecting five navvies *(above)*.
Butterton Station and Swainsley Hall. Note the standard gauge siding *(below)*.

This interesting photo shows the remains of the Ecton Mine dressing floor on the right with the clockhouse smelter at the roadside and a cottage (now demolished) behind it on the bend in the road.

Facing page: Former Ecton mine buildings before the opening of the cheese and milk factory . The entrance to Salts level may be seen plus the Boulton and Watt winding house on the skyline before the roof was lowered. The mine manager's house is on the left but the mine had closed in 1891 *(above).* A similar view after the cheese factory opened. Two low-sided wagons are on the siding adjacent to the buildings *(below).*

ECTON MINES.

An old postcard of Ecton. The man stands between a little chapel built after the mine closed (and where Sir Thomas Wardle played the organ), and the mine's Clockhouse Smelter – it had a clock on the far side *(above)*. Ecton Station with the passing loop and line to the stone loading dock to the right *(below)*.

Manifold Valley.

One of the glass lined bulk milk tankers on the transporter car leaving Ecton *(above)*. One of the tankers in the Creamery siding. The large wooden buffer behind the photographer survived until 1964 *(below)*.

E.R. Calthrop poses for a photograph at the creamery. The milk was bound for United Dairies, Finsbury Park in London. Note the clock face on the old smelter.

Facing page: **E.R. Calthrop** at Hulme End. The bowler hatted gentleman on the left looks like Mr. J.B. Earle. From an old NSR photograph.

Hooper Pumping Station, Manifold Valley.

Coaling at Hulme End. The old coach body was used for storage of parcels and cycles.

Facing page: Early days at Hulme End. Note the carriage shed is open sided.

Hulme End Station from the road in LMS days. The two adverts show the Trooping of the Colour in London.

Facing page: Perhaps the best view of Hulme End Station in later years. Standard gauge rolling stock stand to the left down from the booking office with the engine and coach sheds to the right. Note the travelling gantry, water tank and coal bunker. (Photomatic).

Train in LMS livery with transporter car to the left (*Photomatic*).

Hulme End booking office and storage shed (*Photomatic*).

Above: Hulme End village a hundred years ago.
Below: A horse drawn sleigh between the station and the bridge at Hulme End.

Facing page: Light duties before departure *(Photomatic).*

E.R. Calthrop at Thor's Cave on track removal work in 1937. The line closed from 12th March 1934 and the last train ran amid snow and rain on 10th March.

DEMOLITION

Demolition work at Hulme End *(above)*. The demolition crew pose for a photograph *(below)*.

E.R. Calthrop had definitely seen better days. In fact it had been stored at Waterhouses under canvas for about three years *(above)*. *Real Photos.* The train at Redhurst Crossing *(below)*.

At Waterhouses; the engine looks filthy.

Another view by the old Waterhouses signal box.

One final photocall for the crew at Waterhouses. The old coach behind the men features on the photo below behind the transporter cars *(above)*. The rolling stock stored at Waterhouses *(below)*.

Two depressing views at Waterhouses after the removal of the light railway track. On the upper photo, the old coach was the lamp and porter's rooms. The large building was the main station building and was used as the ladies waiting room, booking hall and office. The rear building was a shelter. The narrow gauge existed in the foreground. The lower photo shows the view looking back from the shelter. *L&GRP. Facing page:* The closure notice.

PUBLIC NOTICE

Notice is hereby given that the

Manifold Valley Light Railway Section

of the Company's Line

WATERHOUSES to HULME END

will be CLOSED for the conveyance of ALL classes of traffic on and from MONDAY, MARCH 12th, 1934

BY ORDER.

District Goods and
    Passenger Manager's Office,
        Stoke-on-Trent.
March 1st, 1934.

The Company have excellent facilities for dealing with PASSENGERS, GOODS and MINERALS Traffic at the following Stations, covering the WATERHOUSES to HULME END area:—

ALSOP-EN-LE-DALE	TISSINGTON
HARTINGTON	WATERHOUSES
IPSTONES	WINKHILL.
THORPE CLOUD	

(R.R.O. 1891.)